TALES OF EDGAR ALLAN POE

TALES OF
EDGAR ALLAN POE

By Edgar Allan Poe

Adapted by Diana Stewart
Illustrated by Charles Shaw

RSVP
RAINTREE
STECK-VAUGHN
PUBLISHERS
The Steck-Vaughn Company

Austin, Texas

Library of Congress Number: 80-14064

Library of Congress Cataloging-in-Publication Data

Stewart, Diana.
  Tales of Edgar Allan Poe.

  (Raintree short classics)
  CONTENTS: The masque of the red death.—The cask of amontillado.—The pit and the pendulum.—The tell-tale heart.—Hop-frog.
  1. Horror tales, American. 2. Children's stories, American. [1. Horror stories. 2. Short stories] I. Poe, Edgar Allan, 1809-1849. II. Shaw, Charles, 1941– III. Title IV. Series.
  PZ7.S84878Tal   [Fic.]   80-14064

ISBN 0-8172-1662-6 hardcover library binding

ISBN 0-8114-6841-0 softcover binding

30 29 28 27 26 25 24 23   07 06 05

CONTENTS

THE MASQUE OF THE RED DEATH

1

The "Red Death" had long plagued the country. No disease had ever been so deadly or so terrible. Blood was its sign and its seal — the redness and horror of blood. First came sharp pains, sudden dizziness, then bleeding from every pore, and finally death. One look at the bloody stains on a victim's body — especially his face — and he was an outcast. No person dare offer him help or sympathy. The length of the disease, from its beginning to death, was one half hour.

But the Prince Prospero was happy and fearless and shrewd. When half the people in his kingdom had died from the bloody death, he called to him a thousand of his healthy, happy friends. With them he went to the outer limits of his kingdom. There he had a huge, magnificent castle surrounded by a high wall. The gates to the castle were of iron. Once he and his friends were inside, he commanded that the gates be welded shut so no one could leave or enter. With these precautions, the prince's guests could defy the disease. The world outside could take care of itself. In the meantime it was foolish to be sad, or to think. Inside he had gathered everything necessary for their comfort and pleasure. They had food and wine to eat and drink, and musicians, clowns, dancers, and actors to entertain.

Inside was safety. Outside was the "Red Death."

After six months had passed in the castle, Prince Prospero entertained his friends at a masked ball. For the dance the guests dressed themselves in their most lavish costumes. Some came as fairies, some as madmen. Some came to delight, some to terrify. Mixing together at the ball was wit and charm, beauty and ugliness.

But let me tell you about the rooms the Prince had prepared for his dance. There were seven rooms in all, and each had been decorated in a different color. There were no lights or candles in the rooms themselves, but in the wall of each room was a stained-glass window facing the hallway. Behind the window was placed a torch so that the light from the torch shone in the window and thus into the room.

The first room, for example, had blue drapes and carpets, and the window was a bright blue. The second chamber was done in purple — and the window was purple. The third was green throughout — and so was the window. The fourth was orange. The fifth was white. The sixth was violet. The seventh room was hung with black velvet drapes that covered the ceiling and walls and fell onto the black carpet. Only in this room was the window different. The panes of glass were red — a deep blood color. The fire behind the window threw a ghastly red light on the black furnishings within. The look of it was terrible, and few of the guests dared to set foot in the room at all.

Also in this room stood a giant clock of black wood — ebony. Its pendulum swung back and forth with a dull, heavy clang. When the clock struck the hour, the sound of the chime was clear and loud and deep. But there was also a strange note in the sound — so strange that when the hour struck, the musicians stopped their playing to listen, and the dancers stood still in place. The tone was so odd that even the silliest of the guests was silent and grew pale. The wise guests stood quiet and thoughtful. When the chimes had at last died away, the musicians played once more and the dancers began again. Once more there was music and laughter. But each time the hour struck, the same quiet fell over the company.

In spite of these things, it was a gay and wonderful party. The prince's tastes were strange. He had a fine eye for

colors and effects. His plans were bold and fiery. There were some who would have thought him mad. His followers felt sure that he was not. You needed to hear and see and touch him to be *sure* that he was not.

Throughout the evening, the guests moved through the rooms, whirling and dancing. The wild music echoed their steps. In each room the dancers took on the color of the chamber. The music would swell, and the dancers would dance. They moved like dreams from room to room. Then, as the clock struck, they all would freeze, and all would be silent save the voice of the clock. Then when the chimes died away, they would dance once more.

As the evening grew later and later, the company danced in all the rooms but one. Few dared to enter the black room. The red light and black drapery were frightful. Those who stood in the black room heard a louder note from the black clock than those who danced in the other rooms. Those rooms were crowded and beat with the heart of life. The guests danced until midnight arrived.

Then, as before, the music stopped and the dancers were quieted upon the sounding of the clock. But now there were twelve chimes to be sounded. During this time, perhaps, more of thought crept into the minds of the most thoughtful guests. And it was during this time, too, that the guests became aware of a stranger among them. It was a masked figure that no one had noticed before. The news of his presence spread quickly through all the rooms. When the company saw him, there was a murmur of surprise, terror, horror, and disgust.

As I said before, the costumes the guests wore were a mixture of the beautiful and the ugly, but the stranger's dress frightened them all.

Even in an easy, carefree group such as this, there were some things that could not be joked about. And the company was angry at the joke the stranger played on them — for this is how he looked to them:

His figure was tall and thin and dressed from head to foot in a shroud — the robe of a dead person ready for the grave.

The mask that covered his face was made to look like a corpse. All this would have been accepted and approved — but the stranger went too far. He had gone so far, in fact, as to have his mask take on the look of the Red Death. His clothes were covered in blood, and his face was sprinkled with the red terror.

Back and forth the stranger moved through the dancers. When Prince Prospero saw him, he shuddered in fear and disgust. Then, his face turned red with rage.

"Who dares," the Prince demanded, "Who dares insult us like this? Seize him and unmask him. Let us know who makes fools of us. Tomorrow we will hang him from the tower!"

Prince Prospero stood in the first of the seven rooms, but his voice rang loud and clear through all seven. But no one moved. The guests watched horrified as the stranger walked slowly and carefully among them. No one dared put out a hand to stop him. They moved back away, against the walls as he passed within a yard of the Prince and down the center of each room.

First through the blue room he went. Then through the purple, through the green to the orange he walked. From there to the white and on to the violet he moved. Not until he entered the last room — the black room — did anyone move to stop him.

It was the Prince himself, finally, who hurried after the unwelcome guest — through the six chambers. He was maddened with rage and ashamed of his own cowardice. On and on he ran, his dagger raised.

At last he reached the black chamber and stood within three feet of the figure. Suddenly the man turned and faced the Prince. There was a sharp cry, and the dagger dropped onto the black carpet. Instantly afterward, the Prince himself fell — dead.

In wild despair, the guests crowded into the black room and threw themselves on the tall figure standing straight and still in front of the ebony clock. But with a cry they drew back. The body and mask they tried to hold belonged to no man but to a ghost. And they knew the stranger for what he was — the Red Death.

The Red Death had come like a thief in the night. And one by one the company dropped to the blood-stained floor. Each died in the position of his fall. And the life of the ebony clock went out with the last man. And the flames behind the windows went out. And darkness and decay and the Red Death ruled over all.

THE CASK OF AMONTILLADO

2

Fortunato had injured me a thousand times. These un-kindnesses I put up with as best I could. But when he insulted me, I vowed to have my revenge. I did not, of course, tell him. I would take my time and plan my revenge well.

Revenge would be no good if I ran the risk of being punished. Nor would there be any pleasure in revenge if Fortunato did not know that I was the one who avenged the wrongs he had done me.

So I smiled in his face, and he did not know that I smiled at the thought of his death.

Now, Fortunato was a man both respected and feared. But he had a weakness. He prided himself on being an expert in wine. I also was considered something of an expert, and I bought fine wines whenever I could.

Time passed, and carnival season arrived. It was a time for drinking and dancing and merriment and pleasure. About dusk on the night I had planned for my revenge, I met Fortunato. He greeted me warmly, for he had been drinking a great deal. He was dressed in motley — the costume of the court fool — with tight-fitting, two-colored pants and a cap with bells.

"My dear Fortunato," I said. "How glad I am to see you. I have a new cask of wine. I was told that the wine was Amontillado, but I have my doubts."

"What?" Fortunato replied. "Amontillado? A whole cask in the middle of carnival season? Impossible!"

"I have my doubts," I repeated, "and I don't want to pay the price for Amontillado if the wine is an imitation. I wanted to ask your opinion, but I could not find you."

"Amontillado?" he asked again.

"Since you were not at home, I was on my way to see Luchresi. I will ask his opinion."

"Luchresi cannot tell Amontillado from Sherry!"

"Yet some people say his taste in wine is as good as your own," I said.

"Come, let us go," Fortunato said curtly.

"Where?"

"To your vaults."

"My friend, no. I could not ask that of you when you are busy. Luchresi —"

"Luchresi could tell you nothing! Come, let us go." And thus saying, he took my arm and hurried me toward my house.

There were no servants at home. I had told them I would be gone all night, and I gave them orders not to leave the house. Such an order was enough to make sure that they would leave as soon as my back was turned.

I took a torch from its holder and handed another one to Fortunato. I then led the way down a long, winding stair that led to the vaults below — the vaults where members of my family had been buried for centuries.

My friend's steps were unsteady, and the bells on his cap jingled as he walked. As we entered the cold, damp air of the vaults under the house, Fortunato began to cough.

"How long have you had this cough?" I asked, but he continued to cough and could not answer for several minutes.

"It is nothing," he said at last.

"Come," I said. "We will go back. Your health is precious. You are rich, respected, admired, beloved. You are ill, and I cannot be responsible. Besides, there is Luchresi —"

"Enough!" he cried. "The cough is nothing. It will not kill me. I shall not die of a cough."

"True, true," I replied. "Here. Have some wine. It will warm you." And I broke the neck off a bottle of wine from the shelf. "Drink."

He raised it to his lips and the bells on his cap jingled. "I drink," he said, "to the dead buried around us."

"And to your long life," I replied.

He again took my arm, and we continued on. "These vaults," he said, "are large."

"I come from a large family — a large and noble family."

"What is your family crest?"

"It is a human foot crushing a snake."

"And the motto?" he asked.

"No man insults us without punishment."

"Very good!" he replied.

The wine sparkled in his eyes and the bells jingled. Down and down through the vaults we walked. We passed through long walls lined with piles of skeletons. Casks of wine stood between the piles. Down we went to the deepest, darkest part of the vault.

I seized Fortunato by the arm above his elbow. "We are below the river now," I said. "See? The drops of water trickle among the bones. Come, we will go back. Your cough —"

"It is nothing!" he said. "Let us go on. But first, another drink of wine."

I reached up and broke open another bottle for him. He emptied it in one breath. His eyes flashed, and he laughed, throwing the bottle upwards.

"Do you understand why I did that?" he asked. "Are you of the brotherhood? Are you a mason?"

"Yes," I replied. "Here is my sign." And I reached beneath the folds of my robe and removed a trowel.

"You are joking!" he said. "But come, let us see the Amontillado."

He leaned heavily on me. We continued our search for the Amontillado. At last we came to a shallow hole in the wall — a burial crypt — about four feet deep, three feet wide, and six feet high. Bones lay all around the opening.

"There!" I said. "In there is the Amontillado."

He staggered forward into the crypt but stopped when he reached the stone wall inside. In an instant I had him chained to an iron ring set in the rocks. I wrapped the chain around his arms and his waist and locked the chains with a padlock. He was too surprised and drunk to resist me.

"Feel how damp the walls are, Fortunato," I said. "Once again I must beg you to return. No? Then I am afraid I must leave you. But I will give you all the attention in my power."

Saying this, I pushed a pile of bones aside and uncovered a supply of building stone and mortar. With these and my trowel I began to wall up the entrance to the hole. I had barely finished the first layer of stone when I heard Fortunato cry out, and I knew that the effects of the wine had worn off.

I laid the second and third layers and heard the chains rattle. I stopped my work and sat down on a pile of bones so I could listen to the sounds of his fear with pleasure. When they stopped, I began my work once more.

Five, six, seven layers I put in place. The wall was now nearly up to my breast. I paused again and held the torch up so I could see the man inside.

Loud, shrill screams rang through the vault. For a moment I hesitated. I trembled. But my strength quickly returned, and I echoed his screams with my own until he was silent, and all grew still and quiet.

It was now midnight, and my work was nearly done. I finished the eighth, ninth, tenth layer, and part of the eleventh. One single stone remained to be fitted into place. Now from out of the crypt came a low laugh and then a voice.

"Ha, ha, ha! — a very good joke!" the voice said. "We shall laugh about this over our wine."

"The Amontillado?" I asked.

"Yes, the Amontillado! But it is getting late. Let us be gone."

"Yes," I said. "Let us be gone."

"For the love of God!" Fortunato cried — and then he was silent.

"Fortunato!" I called, but there was no answer. "Fortunato!" I repeated. No answer still. I thrust the torch through the remaining space and let it fall. From within I heard only the jingle of the bells.

I hurried to finish my work. I forced the last stone into place and plastered it up. Against the new wall I once again placed the pile of bones.

For half a century no person has disturbed those bones. Rest in peace, Fortunato!

THE PIT AND THE PENDULUM

3

I was sick — sick to death of the long agony of waiting. At last I saw the lips of the black-robed judges move as they spoke my fate. The sentence of the Inquisition — the dreaded sentence of death — was the last thing I heard. Then came the silence, the stillness, the blackness. I had fainted.

I seemed to dream for a long time. I remember tall figures who lifted me and carried me down, down, and still down. When my mind awoke from its deep sleep, memory returned, and with it came all the terrors — the trial, the judges, the sentence of death. Slowly my physical senses returned. I lay on my back, and I could feel the anxious beating of my heart, the sound of it in my ears. I reached out a hand, and it fell heavily on the damp, stone floor.

Slowly I opened my eyes and saw — nothing! All was dark. Not a crack of light showed me my prison, and a terrible idea entered my head. My blood pounded in my ears. Was this a tomb? Had I been buried alive? I threw my arms wildly above and around me in all directions. I felt nothing.

The agony of suspense became unbearable. Cautiously I stood and moved forward for a few steps — my hands out in front of me. Still nothing! And I breathed more easily. I was alive, and this was not a tomb.

Now as I walked slowly forward, a thousand thoughts poured into my brain. I remembered stories I had heard of the horrors that took place in this Spanish prison. Terrible stories they were — too ghastly to repeat. What was to be *my* fate? Had I been left to starve in this black dungeon? Or did some more horrible death await me?

At last my hands met a wall — smooth, slimy and cold. I started walking carefully, remembering the old stories of these dungeons. Walking, however, left me no way to find out the size of my prison. I might walk completely around and return to the point where I started without knowing it. I thought of the knife which had been in my pocket, but it was gone; my clothes had been exchanged for a wrapper of coarse cloth. I had thought of forcing the knife into some tiny crack to mark my position. That problem, though, was easily overcome. I tore a piece of cloth from my robe and placed it at right angles to the wall. I could not help but feel it as I finished walking. Carefully I started along the wall, trying to figure the size of my prison. I had taken fifty-two steps when weakness overcame me. I stumbled, fell, and once again fainted.

Upon awakening, I stretched out my arm. Beside me I found a loaf of bread and a pitcher of water. Hungrily I ate and drank before continuing my tour of the walls. Now I decided to try walking straight across the dungeon. At first I moved with great caution, for the floor was slick with slime. Finally, I gained courage and began to walk firmly. I had not gone more than ten or twelve steps, however, when I caught my foot in the torn hem of my robe and fell heavily on my face.

It took me a moment to notice that something was strange. Then I was aware that my chin rested on the floor of the prison, but my lips, nose and forehead touched nothing. At the same time, I smelled the odor of dampness and decay.

I put forward my arm, and shuddered to find that I had fallen on the very edge of a round hole — a pit. Carefully I removed a loose stone from the rim of the pit and let it fall into the opening. I listened as it hit against the sides of the well, and then from far below me came the splash of water echoing through the pit.

At the same moment, a door opened and closed above me, and a faint gleam of light flashed through the darkness. Quickly it faded away, but for a moment I saw clearly the death that had been prepared for me. If I had taken another step, I would have plunged into the pit. I was saved by my fall.

Shaking in every limb, I felt my way back to the wall, and at last I slept.

When I awoke, I found again a loaf of bread and a pitcher of water. I was burning with thirst and drank the water in one breath. But it must have been drugged, for when I drank, I fell into a deep sleep.

I have no idea, of course, how long I slept, but when I opened my eyes, a dim light glowed in the room. For the first time I could see my prison. The pit was in the center of a twenty foot square room. The walls were not smooth stone as I had thought. They were made of sheets of metal and were painted with horrible scenes of death. Devils, ghosts, and skeletons all performed acts of bloody torture.

I saw all this clearly, but with great effort — for I had been moved while I slept. I now lay tightly bound on a low, wooden bed. Several layers of rope went around my body and the wooden frame. Only my head and left arm were free. With this arm, I could just reach the bowl of food placed on the floor beside me. I saw, to my horror, that the pitcher had been removed. I say to my horror, because I was terribly thirsty. To make it worse, the meat in the dish was highly seasoned.

Looking upward, I saw the ceiling of my prison. It was about thirty or forty feet overhead and made of metal like the walls. In the center of it was painted the figure of Father Time. In his hand he held a huge pendulum, like those in old clocks.

Suddenly I looked at the drawing more carefully. I thought for a moment that the pendulum was moving. As I watched, I saw that it was not my imagination. The pendulum did move — back and forth, very slowly.

A slight noise below me drew my attention. I glanced at

the floor and saw several rats crawling up out of the black pit. They came with hungry eyes, drawn by the smell of the meat in the bowl. With my free hand, I drove them away from my food.

Perhaps an hour passed before I looked at the ceiling again. What I saw puzzled and amazed me. The movement of the pendulum was more obvious now. Back and forth it swung. To my horror I saw that it was lower than before and was very, very slowly coming nearer and nearer to me. I could see now that the end of the pendulum was made of steel. It was shaped in a half circle, curving upward on the sides. And even in the dim light I could tell that the bottom edge was very thin and sharp as a razor. Now I could hear the hissing sound it made as it swung through the air.

At last I knew the death planned for me! The pendulum hung so that the razor-sharp edge would swing across my body — across my chest and finally through my heart! I had escaped falling into the pit, so another torture had been planned — a slow, terrible torture!

Inch by inch the pendulum lowered. Down — steadily down it crept. And the lower it came, the farther it swung. It nearly reached the sides of my prison walls. To the right — to the left — far and wide it hissed through the air. Hours passed and the waiting was its own torture.

I laughed. I cried. I prayed until I wearied heaven with my prayers as down, ever down the pendulum came. Down — still down it crept. I took a strange pleasure in watching its speed. It swung with a horrible shriek; it neared my heart with the stealthy pace of the tiger!

Now it swung within three inches of my heart.

I was sick and weak. Even with this terror above me, I craved food. Painfully I reached out my left arm as far as I could. Carefully I took a small piece of meat that the rats had not eaten.

Down — down came the pendulum. I shrank back. My eyes followed it as it swung. I shuddered in terror, and suddenly knew that death would be a relief. But even as I thought this, I was filled with a strange hope. For the first time since my torture began, my brain was clear and alert. I had an idea! I could see the rope that tied me down. It was a single rope wrapped around my body. If the first stroke of the pendulum would cut through it, with my left hand I could free the rest of my body.

Would my plan work? Fearfully I raised my head to look at the rope. My heart dropped. The ropes were tied all around my body — except in the path of the deadly pendulum.

Wearily, I lay my head back down. The pendulum continued to swing. Hissss. Hissss. Another ten or twelve times and it would reach my chest.

The only other sound in the room was the swarm of rats that covered the floor. They were wild and bold and hungry. Their red eyes gleamed up at me as they waited. Waited for what? My blood and flesh!

"What food," I thought, "have they been eating in the pit?"

My hand hung over the side of the wooden frame. It was covered with the oil from the meat I had eaten, and one of the rats sank his teeth into my finger. I was suddenly struck with another idea.

Carefully I brushed the animals away from the bowl. Nothing was left in it now but the meat juice. I covered my hand with it. Bringing up my dripping fingers, I rubbed the juice and oil on the rope wherever I could reach it. Then, I lay back — quiet, not moving.

At first the rats remained still. Then one of the boldest leaped up on the wooden frame. It smelled at the juice on the rope. This seemed a signal for the others. They came from everywhere. Hundreds of them leaped onto the frame. They clung to the wood. They climbed on my body. I could feel them on my arms, my chest, my throat, my face. I could feel their cold lips against mine. They stayed out of the way of the swinging pendulum, chewing on the juice-covered rope. My heart pounded. I nearly fainted from the horror of the rats.

Just when I thought I could not stand it any longer, I felt

the ropes give way. One minute I was tied — the next I was free. The ropes hung loose around my body. But the stroke of the pendulum was on me. It cut through my robes. It cut through the linen beneath. Twice more it swung, and I felt pain. The moment to escape had come. I waved my hand, and the rats ran. As the pendulum swung to the far wall, I slid out from under the last of the ropes. The pendulum swung back again — but it missed me. I was free!

Immediately the pendulum stopped swinging. It was drawn up through the ceiling. I knew then that I was being watched. I was free of the pendulum but not free from the terror of death. I had only traded one kind of torture for another yet unknown.

A minute passed, and then another. Cautiously I looked around. The walls drew my attention. Some change had taken place in the room. I became aware, for the first time, of the origin of the dim light which lit the cell. It came from a crack, about a half an inch in width, which ran around the prison at the base of the walls. The walls were completely separated from the floor. When I had first noticed them, the paintings had been dim and faded. Now they glowed with a strange, red light. The devils' eyes gleamed with fire! I panted. I gasped for breath. I could smell the hot metal of the walls, and I knew what death was planned for me next.

The heat from the walls drove me to the center of the room — to the edge of the pit. I could now see into it. For a moment, I refused to believe what I saw. Oh, for a voice to speak! Oh! any horror but this! With a cry I ran from the edge, weeping.

My prison grew hotter and hotter. I heard the sound of scraping metal. As I watched, the room began to change its shape. The walls on each side of me were beginning to move. They came in closer and closer towards me. They pressed onward, driving me into the pit. At last for my burned body there was no longer an inch of foothold on the floor of the prison. My soul cried out in one loud, long, and final scream of agony and despair. I teetered on the edge of the pit —

Suddenly came the hum of voices! There was the loud blast of many trumpets! The fiery walls rushed back! An arm caught my own as I fell fainting toward the pit.

It was a soldier who saved me. The French army had entered the city. The Inquisition was at an end. Toledo was in the hands of its enemies.

THE TELL-TALE HEART

4

True! It is true that I had been very, very nervous. I am still nervous, but why will you say that I am mad? The disease merely sharpened my senses. Above all, it made my sense of hearing very strong. I heard all things in the heaven and in the earth. I heard many things in hell. Why, then, do you think I am mad? Listen and see how calmly I tell you the whole story.

I cannot say when the idea first entered my brain, but once it had, it haunted me day and night. I had no reason for my crime. I did not hate the old man. In fact, I loved him. He had never hurt me. He had never insulted me. I did not want his money. I think it was his eye! Yes, that was it! He had the eye of a vulture. It was pale blue — with a film over it. Whenever he looked at me with that pale, blue eye my blood ran cold. So, as time passed, I decided to kill the old man and get rid of the eye forever.

Now you think I am mad. But madmen don't know what they are doing. You should have seen me. You should have seen how wisely I began my work.

For the whole week before I killed the old man, I was very kind to him. But every night at midnight, I opened the door to his room — oh, so gently! I opened it until I could just fit my head inside. Oh, you would have laughed to see how carefully and quietly I worked so I did not awaken him. I moved my head slowly — very, very slowly. It took me an hour to put my whole head in the narrow opening so I could see him on his bed.

Ha! Would a madman have been so wise?

When my head was in the room, I held up a closed lantern. I undid its door cautiously — oh, so cautiously. I undid it just so a single ray of light fell on the vulture eye.

And I did this every night for seven long nights — every night just at midnight. But each night I found the eye closed. I could not do my work when the eye was closed, because I did not hate the old man — only his Evil Eye.

Every morning I would go in to him. I would greet him warmly and ask how he had slept. He never knew that each night I watched him in his sleep.

On the eighth night, I was more careful than ever. Never had I felt so powerful or so wise. There I was, opening the door very quietly. And the old man did not even dream of my secret thoughts. I nearly laughed at the idea. Perhaps I did laugh. Perhaps he heard me, for suddenly he moved on the bed.

Now you may think that I drew back. But no! His room was black. The shutters were closed. I knew he could not see the door opening, and I kept pushing it inward.

I had my head in and started to open the lantern, but my finger slipped. The old man sprang up in bed, crying out: "Who's there?"

I kept quite still and said nothing. For a whole hour I did not move a muscle, and I did not hear him lie down. He was sitting very still in his bed listening.

At last I heard a slight groan. It was not a groan of pain or of grief. Oh, no! It was the low sound that comes from the bottom of a man's soul when he is filled with terror. I knew the sound well. Many was the time I had felt just such terror in my life. I knew what the old man felt. I pitied him, but I laughed in my heart. He had been lying there awake, and his fears had grown in him. He had been saying to himself: "It is nothing but the wind. It is only a mouse crossing the floor. It is merely a cricket."

Yes, he had been trying to comfort himself — but he could not. He could not because Death was coming nearer and nearer to him from out of the shadows. Although he

could hear and see nothing — he felt the presence of Death.

When I had waited a long time, and he still did not lay back down, I carefully opened the lantern. The single ray of light now fell full upon the vulture eye.

The eye was wide, wide open, and I grew angry as I looked at it. I saw it clearly — all dull and blue — with the ugly film over it that chilled my bones. I could not see anything of the old man — only the blue eye.

I told you in the beginning that I was not mad. I just had a strong power of hearing. Now, there came to my ears a low, dull, quick sound. I knew that sound well. It was the beating of the old man's heart. Still I kept quiet, keeping the ray of light on the eye. Meantime, the old man's heart beat faster and faster, louder and louder. He was terrified. It grew louder, I say, louder every moment — do you hear me? I thought the heart would burst.

I have told you that I am nervous. So I am. As the heart beat louder, I became frightened. What if the neighbors heard it?

The time for the old man's death had come! With a loud yell, I threw open the door of the lantern and leaped into the room. He screamed once — only once. In an instant I dragged him to the floor and pulled the heavy bed over him. For many minutes the heart continued to beat, but this did not trouble me. The bed muffled the sound, and it would not be heard through the wall. At last the heartbeat stopped. The old man was dead. I removed the bed and looked at the dead body. Yes, he was stone, stone dead. I placed my hand on the heart and held it there. Yes, he was dead. I smiled happily. I had done my work. The eye would never trouble me again!

If you still think I am mad, you will not think so when I tell you what I did next. I worked quietly and quickly. First of all, I cut up the corpse. I cut off the head and the arms and the legs.

Then I took up three boards from the floor of the room. Into the hole I put the parts of the old man's body. I then replaced the boards so cleverly, so carefully, that no eye —

not even his — could have seen anything wrong. There were no blood stains. I was too careful for that. I had caught all the blood in a tub — ha! ha!

When I finished my work, it was four o'clock and still dark. As the clock struck the hour, a knock came at the street door. I went down to open it with a happy heart. Why should I worry? I had nothing to fear.

Three men entered. They were policemen. A scream had been heard by a neighbor during the night. The police had been sent to find out if anything was wrong.

I smiled and welcomed the gentlemen in. The scream, I said, was my own. I had had a nightmare. The old man was away in the country. I led my visitors all over the house. I invited them to search. At last I took them to the old man's chamber. I showed them his treasures — all safe. I brought in chairs and invited them to rest for a few minutes.

Excited and pleased with myself, I placed my own chair over the very spot where the corpse of my victim lay.

The police were satisfied. I convinced them that all was well by my smiling face and easy manner. They stayed, and I answered all their questions cheerfully. We talked of other subjects. But before long, I felt myself getting pale, and I wished they would leave. My head ached, and I heard a ringing in my ears. But still they sat and talked. The sound became louder and louder, and soon I knew that the noise was not in my own head.

No doubt I now grew very pale, but I talked on and on. I now heard the sound clearly. It was a low, dull, quick sound, like the beating of a heart. I gasped for breath, but the policemen did not hear it. I talked more quickly. But the noise became louder and louder. I stood and walked around the room.

Why didn't they leave!

Back and forth I walked the floor. God! What could I do! I foamed at the mouth — I shouted — I swore! And the sound grew louder — louder — louder!

And still the men sat, smiling and talking. The men must have heard the heartbeat. They heard! They knew! They knew what I had done! They were mocking me. I was in agony. I couldn't stand their knowing smiles any longer. I felt that I must scream or die! And now — again — listen! Louder! Louder! Louder! — the heart beat!

"Villains!" I cried. "You know! You know! I admit the crime! Tear up the boards — here, here! It is the beating of his heart — his ugly heart!"

HOP–FROG

5

I never knew anyone who loved a joke as much as the king. He seemed to live only for joking. To tell a good joke was the surest way to win his favor. Thus it was that his seven ministers were all known for their skill as jokers. They all took after the king. They were large, fat, oily men, and they loved a good joke. The king and his ministers liked a good, funny story, but they loved a good practical joke most of all.

Now in the largest and most powerful kingdoms, the kings kept court jesters — fools dressed in motley with a cap and bells. These jesters were expected to keep the king entertained with smart sayings and jokes.

Our king, too, had his fool. Only his jester was worth three times as much as any other, because he was a dwarf and a cripple. His name was Hop-Frog. The king gave him the name because the dwarf could not walk as other men do. In fact, Hop-Frog could only get around by a sort of strange step — something between a leap and a wriggle. And this strange movement gave the king and his ministers a good many laughs.

But although Hop-Frog could only move along the ground with great pain and difficulty, his arms were very strong. He could perform many wonderful tricks in the trees or on ropes, and he could climb anything with the use of his arms alone. When he was climbing and swinging thus, he looked more like a small monkey than a frog.

I cannot say exactly where Hop-Frog came from. He and a young girl dwarf had been taken prisoner during a war

with a far-off country. The general of the army had given the two dwarfs to the king as gifts.

While Hop-Frog was twisted and deformed, Trippetta — for that was the name of the girl — was graceful and beautiful. Hop-Frog and Trippetta were alone in the strange kingdom, and they became great friends. The court laughed at Hop-Frog, but they admired and petted Trippetta for her beauty and skill as a dancer.

When my story begins, the king was giving a masked ball. And the night of the ball had arrived. The whole court had been planning their costumes for weeks. Everyone was ready — everyone, that is, except the king and his seven ministers. They could not make up their minds what costumes to wear. And they sent for the two dwarfs for suggestions.

When Trippetta and Hop-Frog went to the king, they found him drinking wine with his ministers. The king was in a bad temper. He knew that Hop-Frog did not like wine. It nearly drove the poor cripple mad. But the king loved his practical jokes, and he took pleasure in forcing Hop-Frog to drink.

"Come here, Hop-Frog," the king said as the jester and Trippetta entered. "Drink this glass of wine. Drink to the health of your friends at home. Then tell us how to dress tonight — something new and different. Come, drink!"

Hop-Frog tried to refuse the wine with a joke, but he couldn't. It happened that it was the poor dwarf's birthday, and the mention of his friends at home brought tears to his eyes. Many large, bitter tears fell into the glass as he took it from the king.

"Ha! ha! ha!" roared the king as the dwarf drank the wine. "See what a glass of good wine can do? Why, your eyes are shining already!"

Poor fellow! His large eyes gleamed with tears.

"Now come, Hop-Frog," the king said. "What do you suggest for our costumes tonight?"

"I am trying to think," Hop-Frog replied.

"Trying to think!" cried the king. "Ah, I see. You want

more wine. Here, drink this!" And he poured another glass. But Hop-Frog did not take it. He just stared at it, gasping for breath.

"Drink, I say!" shouted the king.

When Hop-Frog did not take the glass, the king grew purple with rage. The ministers laughed. Trippetta fell to her knees at the king's feet.

"Please, sire," she said. "Spare my friend."

The king looked at her for a moment. How dare she interfere? Then, without saying a word, he pushed her to the floor and threw the wine in her face. The poor girl got up as best she could and moved away.

There was a dead silence for half a minute. It was interrupted by a low, harsh, grating sound that seemed to come from every corner of the room.

"What is that noise?" the king asked.

"It must be a parrot at the window," one minister replied.

Here the dwarf laughed and showed a set of large, powerful, and very ugly teeth. Now he swallowed as much wine as the king wished — and the king was happy. When the dwarf finished, he gave his suggestion for the costumes.

"I do not know if you will like the idea," he said, his eyes glowing strangely, "but *just after* your majesty had struck the girl and thrown the wine in her face — *just after* your majesty had done this, and while the parrot was making that odd noise outside the window, there came into my mind a wonderful idea. Unfortunately, however, it would need eight people, and —"

"Here we are!" cried the king. "Eight! My seven ministers and myself. Come! Tell us what you are planning?"

"I call it," replied the cripple, "the Eight Chained Apes, and it really is a wonderful joke if it is done well."

"We will do it well!" cried the king.

"The beauty of this joke," continued Hop-Frog, "is the fright it gives the women."

"Marvelous!" roared the king and his ministers.

"Then I will dress you as apes," said the dwarf. "Leave it all to me. The costumes will be so good that the company will take you for real beasts — and, of course, they will be terrified."

"Oh, that is wonderful!" exclaimed the king.

"Once you are in your costumes, I will drape you in chains. You can jangle them and make a great deal of noise. The Eight Chained Apes will rush into the ballroom with terrible cries. The company will believe that you have escaped from your keepers. Your majesty, just imagine the scare you will give your guests!"

And this is how Hop-Frog dressed the eight men. No one had ever seen a real ape, and the dwarf made costumes that were more ugly than true to nature.

First, he had the king and his ministers put on tight-fitting pants and shirts. He then covered them with black tar. Over the tar he put a thick layer of straw. The straw, he said, would look just like the fur of the ape. Next he brought in the chain. He tied it around the waist of the king, and then around the first minister, and then the next. At last all eight men were chained together in a circle. Finally, he crossed the chain in the middle of the circle to form an X.

The grand ballroom was a large, round room. During the day the only light came from a window — a sky-light — set in the very center of the high ceiling. At night the light came from a chandelier that hung from a chain down through the sky-light.

As always, preparing the room for a ball was Trippetta's job. This time, she and Hop-Frog planned the decorations together. They removed the chandelier and placed torches and candles all around the walls of the room. The scene was set for the arrival of the Eight Chained Apes.

Taking Hop-Frog's advice, the king and the ministers waited until midnight before they appeared. No sooner had the clock struck the hour, when in rushed the apes. The horror of the guests filled the king's heart with joy. Several women fainted with fright at the sight of the wild

beasts. Many people made a rush for the door, but the dwarf had locked it as soon as the king entered.

With all the yelling and screaming and rattling of chains, no one noticed that the chain which usually held the chandelier came down out of the sky-light into the center of the room. A large hook was on the end of it. When the king and his ministers reached the middle of the room, Hop-Frog took the hook and put it through the crossed chains in the center of the circle of apes. In an instant the hook was drawn upward and out of reach. The chain dragged the men close together until they stood face to face.

By this time, the company began to see that this was all one of the king's jokes. They set up a shout of laughter.

"Leave them to me!" now screamed Hop-Frog. "I think I know them. If I can only get a good look at them, I can soon tell who they are."

He took a torch from the wall, and like a monkey he jumped on the king's head and climbed up the chain. He held the torch down to look at the apes.

"I shall soon find out who they are!" he screamed.

And now, the whole group — apes included — were doubled up in laughter. Suddenly the dwarf gave a sharp whistle. Up went the hook. The chain was dragged through the roof until the men were hanging between the sky-light and the floor. Hop-Frog stayed clinging to the chain just above them.

A dead silence fell over the crowd. This silence was broken by the same low, harsh, grating noise that the king heard when he threw the wine in Trippetta's face. Now, however, there could be no question where the sound came from. It came from the fang-like teeth of the dwarf. He ground and gnashed his teeth until he foamed at the mouth. His eyes burned with rage as he looked down into the faces of the king and his ministers.

"Ha!" he said at last. "I begin to see who these people are!" Here he thrust the torch down and pretended to look at the king more closely. Then he held the torch to the straw-covered clothes, and instantly they burst into flame.

In less than a minute the whole eight apes were blazing with fire. Below the guests watched horrified — unable to do anything to help them.

As the flames grew higher and higher, the dwarf climbed up the chain. At the top, he stopped and spoke: "Now I see what these men are. They are a king and his seven ministers. A king who strikes a helpless girl and his ministers who laugh with him. As for myself, I am simply Hop-Frog, the fool — and this is my last joke!"

Both the tar and the straw burned quickly, and by the time he had finished his brief speech, his revenge was complete. Eight corpses swung in their chains — a black, hideous, smelling mass. The cripple threw his torch at them, climbed casually up to the ceiling, and disappeared through the sky-light.

It is supposed that Trippetta, waiting on the roof, had helped him in his revenge. Probably the two dwarfs escaped to their own country together — for neither was seen again.

GLOSSARY

chandelier (shan' də liər') a branched light that hangs from the ceiling

Inquisition (in' kwə zish' ən) a Catholic group of thirteenth to sixteenth century Europe. It was set up to find and punish people who spoke against church beliefs.

mason (mas' ən) a person who builds with stone, brick, or cement. Also can mean a member of a secret group called Freemasons.

masque (mask') a short play in which the actors wear masks

minister (min' is tər) a person who is in charge of part of the government

pendulum (pen' jə ləm) a weight that is hung from a fixed point and can swing back and forth

vault (vȯlt') a closed room that can be used for burying bodies